The
Moon
Reflected
Fire

The
Moon
Reflected
Fire

poems by
Doug Anderson

*For Jousie
are one best,
Doug [signature]*

ALICE JAMES BOOKS
Cambridge, Massachusetts

Acknowledgments

Grateful acknowledgement is made to the following journals
in which some of these poems appeared, or will appear.

Ploughshares: "Doc," "Rain" and "Recovery."
Virginia Quarterly Review: "Near Tam Ky 1967" and "Judgment."
Massachusetts Review: "Infantry Assault," "The Wall," "Itinerary" and "Blues."
Southern Review: "Los Desastres de la Guerra" and "Prisoners Song."
Connecticut River Review: "Purification."
North Essex Review: "Mugging, Brooklyn, 1981."
River City: "Bamboo Bridge," "We Sweat" and "Ambush."
Poet & Critic: "Night Ambush" and "Monsoon."
Peregrine: "Xin Loi" and "Yes."
Amherst Writers & Artists Press, Amherst Massachusetts, April 1991: a
chapbook, *Bamboo Bridge*, containing: "Night Ambush," "Infantry Assault,"
"Doc," "Bamboo Bridge,"" Ambush," "We Sweat," "Mine,"" Xin Loi,"
"Prisoner's Song," "Short Timer," "Purification," "Los Desastres de La Guerra,"
"Outliving Our Ghosts," "Yes," "Phantom," "The Wall, Rain," and "Recovery."

Library of Congress Catalog Number: 94-26156
ISBN 1 882 295 03X

Cover and text design by Charles Casey Martin
Cover Art: James Abbott McNeill Whistler,
Nocturne in Black and Gold, The Falling Rocket, (c. 1875),
© The Detroit Institute of Arts, Gift of Dexter M. Ferry, Jr.

Epigraphs: Part I: *The Gospel According to Thomas,* New York: Harper and
Row Publishing, Inc. 1959, Logian 45.
Edward II, by Bertolt Brecht, *Collected Plays of Bertolt Brecht,* New York:
Grove Atlantic Press, 1961.
The Golden Bough, by James Fraser, New York: Avenel Books, 1981.

Alice James Books gratefully acknowledges support from the National
Endowment for the Arts and from the Massachusetts Cultural Council, a
state agency whose funds are recommended by the Governor, and
appropriated by the State Legislature.

Alice James Books are published by the Alice James Poetry Cooperative, Inc.
Look House
University of Maine
Main Street
Farmington, ME 04938

for the Vietnamese and Americans
who knew this war

Table of Contents

If you bring forth what is within you,
what you bring forth will save you.
If you do not bring forth what is within you,
what you do not bring forth will destroy you.
—from the Gospel of Thomas, Logian 45

PART ONE

NIGHT AMBUSH

We are still, lips swollen with mosquito bites.
A treeline opens out onto paddies
quartered by dikes, a moon in each,
and in the center, the hedged island of a village
floats in its own time, ribboned with smoke.
Someone is cooking fish.
Whispers move across water.
Children and old people. Anyone between
is a target. It is so quiet
you can hear a safety clicked off
all the way on the other side.
Things live in my hair. I do not bathe.
I have thrown away my underwear.
I have forgotten the why of everything.
I sense an indifference larger than anything
I know. All that will remain of us
is rusting metal disappearing in vines.
Above the fog that clots the hill ahead
a red tracer arcs and dims.
A black snake slides off the paddy dike
into the water and makes the moon shiver.

INFANTRY ASSAULT

The way he made that corpse dance
by emptying one magazine after another into it
and the way the corpse's face began to peel off
like a mask because the skull had been shattered, brains
spilled out, but he couldn't stop killing that corpse,
wanted to make damn sure, I thought maybe
he was killing all the ones he'd missed, and

the way they dragged that guy out of the stream,
cut him to pieces, the stream running red
with all the bodies in it, and the way the captain
didn't try to stop them, his silence saying *No Prisoners* and

the way when all the Cong were dead, lined up in rows,
thirty-nine in all, our boys went to work on all the pigs
and chickens in the village until
there was no place that was not red, and

finally, how the thatch was lit, the village burned
and how afterwards we were quiet riding back
on the tracks, watching the ancestral serpent rise
over the village in black coils, and
how our bones knew what we'd done.

DOC

They kill them like flies over there
he had slurred on the bus full
of drunk marines going back to Las Pulgas.
Like flies. Corpsmen,
he was talking about.
Six months later I was a replacement,
saw coffins being loaded onto transports
on the airstrip coming in.
Lived through the first firefight,
the second; had a little bag
of wisdom to croak out
to the fool who would replace me:
Break down your medical kit,
pack the innards in your pockets;
get rid of your pistol,
buy a black market shotgun, greasegun,
anything to make you look like
something other than what you are;
and don't walk behind the radioman
or the squad leader on patrol;
they ambush the center of the column,
and by the way,
a muzzle pointed your way pops flat,
away, it echoes;
the round that gets you you won't hear.

BAMBOO BRIDGE

We cross the bridge, quietly.
The bathing girl does not see us
till we've stopped and gaped like fools.
There are no catcalls, whoops,
none of the things that soldiers do;
the most stupid of us is silent, rapt.
She might be fourteen or twenty,
sunk thigh deep in green water,
her woman's pelt a glistening corkscrew,
a wonder, a wonder she is; I forgot.
For a moment we all hold the same thought,
that there is life in life and war is shit.
For a song we'd all go to the mountains,
eat pineapples, drink goat's milk,
find a girl like this, who cares
her teeth are stained with betel nut,
her hands as hard as feet.
If I can live another month it's over,
and so we think a single thought,
a bell's resonance.
And then she turns and sees us there,
sinks in the water, eyes full of hate;
the trance broken.
We move into the village on the other side.

AMBUSH

In the village we unsling our rifles,
drop our packs, light cigarettes, eat, piss,
sleep fly-covered in the heat.
A round comes by my ear, an angry wasp,
and crabwise I scuttle for a hole that isn't there.
There is shouting everywhere, someone is hit.
I see the lieutenant point his pistol with both hands;
a water buffalo is bearing down on him,
stampeded by the shooting. Beside a cistern,
a monk, saffron robed, squats and laughs.
There is a woman running past
tripping on her ao dai, but no, it's not.
Before I can shout a warning the garment comes unsashed,
instead of womanflesh, an automatic rifle
flashes in an arc, and firing from the hip,
the man runs for his life.
Someone trying to duck smashes my nose with his elbow.
It is now quiet. Seven bodies lie in the village road;
three are ours, more are wounded.
My cigarette not gone halfway I begin to treat them.

JUDGMENT

Near Hoi Ahn, 1967

Pinned down two hours in a Buddhist graveyard
by two barefoot snipers who will not die
no matter how many mortars we walk their way.
They keep moving, the one firing, the other
doubling back where the mortars have already been,
nor are they silenced by the gunship
now squandering rockets
at inkblots flickering between trees.
These wraiths sing with their crack and whine,
   We will die to hold you here
   while the others slip away toward the mountains.
   What will you die for?
Me hunkering behind a pitted tombstone
staring at a skull from a grave churned up by tanks.

MAMASAN

We ride on tanks over the new rice,
break down the dikes so the dirty water
runs in with the clear. They run beside us,
little claw gestures toward their mouths,
This is what we eat you are running over.
We look back without expression.
Mamasan stands in front of the lead tank,
hoe raised over her head.
It is not her time to die. The tank stops,
driver comes out of the hatch to look.
Mamasan makes a sound like an old hinge,
shuffles forward,
breaks the tank's searchlight with her hoe.

XIN LOI

The man and woman, Vietnamese,
come up the hill,
carry something slung between them on a bamboo mat,
unroll it at my feet:
the child, iron gray, long dead,
flies have made him home.
His wounds are from artillery shrapnel.
The man and the woman look as if they are cast
from the same iron as their dead son,
so rooted are they in the mud.
There is nothing to say,
nothing in my medical bag, nothing in my mind.
A monsoon cloud hangs above,
its belly torn open on a mountain.

*Xin Loi (pr. "sin loy") means "I am sorry" in Vietnamese.

PURIFICATION

In Taiwan, a child washes me in a tub
as if I were hers.
At fifteen she has tried to conceal
her age with makeup, says her name is *Cher.*
Across the room,
her dresser has become an altar.
Looming largest,
photos of her three children, one black,
one with green eyes, one she still nurses,
then a row of red votive candles, and in front,
a Buddha, a Christ, a Mary.
She holds my face to her breasts, rocks me.
There is blood still under my fingernails
from the last man who died in my arms.
I press her nipple in my lips,
feel a warm stream of sweetness.
I want to be this child's child.
I will sleep for the first time in days.

MINE

We make the paddy crossing fine,
but fifty meters into the trees,
the man two up in front of me steps on a mine,
loses both legs at the hip, and that's not all.
He's stunned, doesn't know how bad it is.
Can't give him morphine in that much shock.
He'll die if he's lucky.
I have less work than I thought:
the blast's heat has cauterized his wounds.
Quickly I fill out the casualty tag.
I'm bleeding too, a rivulet
of my blood blends with one of his.
When he's gone, I wash my wound.
It's not shrapnel. A shard of his
shattered bone is sticking in my arm.

MONSOON

Knowing the first moonless night they would come for us,
crawling up under the wire, tripping the soggy flares,
seven of us set an ambush in the village at the base
of the hill, deserted except for the old woman
who would not leave ancestral mud. I slept in her hootch,
the only one left with a roof, to keep the radio dry.
Toward midnight the flares woke the roosters and I sat up,
saw the old woman squatting next to me in the false moon,
rocking, whispering through black teeth,
Dien cai dau, dien cai dau, *insane*, and again,
the burst of light, the roosters, dien cai dau,
and the dark came darker still around the dying flare.

PRISONER'S SONG

They drag the prisoner to the stream,
bend his back into a bow,
hold him under by the hair,
yank him up, repeat,
and all the time,
as if he were their lover,
whisper to him in Vietnamese,
till half drowned, he breaks,
points to a hooch.
His interrogators, grinning,
tear his carbine from the thatch.
They wire his wrists behind his back,
chain his ankles to the tank,
drag him over stubble and paddy dikes.
From the rear of the tank,
the interrogators, smoking,
contemplate the stripe of blood
that shoots an azimuth
from Tam Ky to Chu Lai.
The prisoner stands beside his shredded flesh and sings:
    Next life I want to be a woman,
        sit in autumn with my baby by the village well,
        watch the sun's yolk,
        mirrored in a thousand flooded paddies.

PAPASAN

In the monsoon when the heat dropped to ninety
we shivered in our ponchos, sand in our hair,
grit in our teeth, weapons jammed.
We dug ourselves in
in what we thought was an abandoned village
at the base of a mountain
and were startled to see him by the water buffalo,
three-strand beard moving in the wind.
He was eighty (his I.D. said),
wrestling a wooden plow all day
in paddies ruined by a swollen river,
a job for an absent son.
When he saw we planned to stay the night,
he stripped and squatted in the ditch to bathe,
scowled at us who stared at him
in this small privacy.
A Vietnamese would have known to turn his eyes away.

WE SWEAT

in a tiny shrine dug in a mountainside,
mulling how to die. Guerillas prod
the bladed scrub with bayonets,
hack toward us with machetes.
Our Vietnamese guide
fired his rifle accidentally,
squats in the darkness, head down.
If the Cong don't find us,
he's thinking, *we'll* kill him.
But revenge is a game of contemplation
for when the dust has settled.
I turn to the wall: something looks out at me
from beneath the vines. A centipede
moves across its face. The god seems
to have four arms, four legs, breasts and balls.
Something in me stirs.
The gods here are not familiar.
Who knows what prayer provokes.
At this thought the red ants
form a net around my body.
When you cannot scream, pray.

TWO BOYS

They take the new machine gun out of its wrap
in pieces, the flat black barrel, the other
parts, delicate in their oil, plastic stock
like a toy until snapped onto the rest,
pressed against the shoulder of the corporal
with almost white blond hair. He looks around
for something to sight in on. With a grin
the other, darker one points to three
children dawdling to school along a paddy dike.
The first rounds are high and the gunner adjusts,
fires again, the children running now,
the rounds pluming in the wet paddies,
another click and all but one child has made
the safety of the treeline, the other splashing
into the new rice, and as the gunner sights in
on him, this eight year old, with wisdom perhaps
from the dead, yanks off his red shirt, becomes
the same color as the fields, the gunner lowering
the muzzle now, whispering a wistful, *damn.*

BETHESDA

Just below Monkey Mountain we dug in, our backs
to the South China Sea, lay down in soft hollows of sand.
I remembered the gentle world beneath the fear,
a woman's hands, and had myself, quietly, under my poncho.
At dawn we watched the French doctor-priest
from the leprosarium lead his patients down
to bathe sores and stumps in the stinging salt water,
and mingling with the lepers we could see the others,
certainly Cong, smiling, nodding, all bones and tendons,
little pink mouths of shrapnel wounds in tunnel-pale skin.
The priest telling us they brought them in at night, bleeding,
and what was he to do? Quietly we watched
them paddle out to where the green turned dark,
and slowly, one by one we stripped and joined them there.

FREE FIRE ZONE

The eighteen year-old who thinks
Christ is about to rain death on commies
kicks the family altar to pieces in an old mud hut.
We set the charge, roll the det cord
into the sun, chase out the old yellow dog;
but he ambles back into the dark, curls
on the cool dirt floor, tongue dripping.
We laugh and blow it anyway; the numbing flash,
dust unfurling low to the ground,
but in a moment the dog staggers
out of the rubble wagging his whole self,
sits down before us expecting to be fed.
We leave him cans to lick, then go north through red dust.
Villagers begin to rebuild their hootches
from the trash we've left, and when in two weeks
we return, the bamboo we hacked down grown back
chest high; the same dog wobbles out of the shade,
licks the shit off a bare-bottomed brat
and sits lopsided in the sun.

PHOTO, 1967

Your hands, lighting a cigarette, are more suited
to a piano than a rifle. You are shrunk to gristle
from the heat, from the fear that keeps you from
eating more than a mouthful, just enough to keep
you moving to the next village. You have just put
a man into a plastic bag, marvelled at the new tattoo
on the stiffening arm. Except for your height,
your nose, your lack of epicanthus, you could blend in
with the local rice farmers, guerillas by night.
Nothing wasted on this body, as if to say to death,
I come to you poor. I have only this spoonful.
The rest is burnt away by my certain knowledge of you.

SHORT TIMER

Twelve hours before his plane was to lift off for home
he was sitting in the EM club
slugging down Filipino beer.
A sniper round rang through the tin roof,
knocked him off his stool, a near complete flip
before he hit the floor.
Next thing I knew we were lugging him
through the sand toward the sick bay;
him bucking and screaming,
me trying to shield the spurting head,
the sniper bearing down on us,
the others scattering to the perimeter to return fire.
Inside we saw how bad it was.
I syringed the long gash in the parietal with sterile water,
the doctor with a flashlight looking close,
the man saying, *Oh God,* and already the slur,
the drool. He would live. Go home.
Sit the rest of his life in front of a television set.
Back in the EM club they had wiped up the blood
and we could see the stars
through the thirty caliber holes in the roof.
What was in the 20 cc's of brain he lost?
These are the things that can occupy a drunk about to black out.
Somewhere a family, a girlfriend, prepared for his return.
Somewhere a telegram raced toward them into Pacific Time
and the dark that rose like water in his room.

NORTH OF TAM KY, 1967

You were dead when I got there, managed to drag yourself
almost to the treeline across the sandy open place
they planned to kill us in, the clearing I would have to crawl
to get to you, and did, the tracers crossing overhead.
The round caught you dropping to the ground, entering longways
between neck and shoulder, taking the artery, the lung.
I had inside me in those days a circuit-breaker between head
and heart that shut out everything but the clarity of fear.
I felt nothing for you then, rolling you over, looking for
the exit wound, nor when I put my mouth on yours and blew,
hearing the gurgle that told me you had drowned in your own blood.
I knew only the muzzle flashes too close in front, the sniper
cracking on my left and I flipped the switch and went cold,
the same whose wires I tinker with these twenty-three years after,
a filament flickering in the heart and then the blaze of light.

PART TWO
Los Desastres de la Guerra

LOS DESASTRES DE LA GUERRA

For Jack Gilbert

1.
Goya walks to the well,
sees the clay a deeper red under his feet,
peers into a well full of blood,
the moon reflected fire.
He wakes, shakes himself free of the dream,
but the feeling persists.
His cat brings him a bird, drops it at his feet.

2.

On the table: cheese, milk,
the thick black bread that makes him fart.
The light in his window is brilliant:
he thinks of Vermeer.
But now framed are peasants carrying flails,
not headed toward the fields,
and now four more, with mauls and staves.
And from the market square,
muskets firing unevenly, a muffled scream.
Passing his window, a French patrol.
Bonjour, Monsieur, the sergeant says, tips his hat.
When they pass Goya spits into the shadows.

3.
The model, Angela, is late.
More shots from the market.
I do not want this day,
he whispers to himself, opens a bottle of wine,
goes into the garden with a sketchbook,
sits in the cool shade of the high vined walls.
I have provisions, he tells himself,
for a week, longer if I care.
I need not go further than the well.
The vines move in the breeze.

4.
That night he does not sleep.
The owls that call from hill to hill are silent.
No wind, no moon, the stars are masked by haze
as if a lizard's slow eyelid veiled the world.
He thinks of his mother, now dead,
lights a candle,
tugs a moldy canvas from a pile,
regards her face. *Hold to this love,*
he tells himself, *whatever comes.*

5.

Next day he cannot eat.
Splashes water on his face, risks a trip to market.
In the shadow of a building, a circle of peasants
lift their flails and bring them down again,
and again, then by some signal disperse,
hats pulled over faces.
They leave something resembling a man,
knowable by his French tunic,
the face misshapen as if by an angry sculptor.
I do not want this day,
he whispers to himself, turning back.

6 .

Two neighbors are quarreling:
No! Aqui! one shouts.
Goya looks out the window,
sees one neighbor dragging a body by the heels.
The argument concerns whose house he fell before
and therefore who must die if soldiers come,
but they arrive before a settlement.
The men are tied to tethering poles at the fountain,
where they weep, as the soldiers discuss
whether to mutilate them live or kill them first.
Goya retreats into his garden with a bottle of wine,
the vial of poison his mother kept.

7.
There is famine now.
Goya eats all the flowers in his garden,
watches the street through the iron gate.
A young man hacks the arm off a corpse,
avoiding the face: it is a small town after all.
Goya remembers the hen he loved as a boy,
raised from a chick,
the day he watched his mother wring its neck,
fat quivering on her arm,
the chicken before him at dinner.

8.
A French mercenary chases a young girl around the well,
her grandmother hobbling behind, shouting,
Merci de Dios, alto! Mi hija. No! No!,
the soldier tearing off her dress with a single swipe,
the girl moonskinned now,
the soldier holding her by the hair,
fumbling for her breasts,
the grandmother drawing his knife from behind,
driving it into his back
with something that comes from beyond her,
the soldier surprised, then dying; Goya saying,
No quieren, No quieren, comprendez?
And laughter and tears.

9.

His model lives on the other side of the hill.
He leaves in the early morning,
keeping distance from the French patrol in front,
looking over his shoulder for scrub and rocks to hide behind.
He has not seen the girl in weeks, carries with him
perhaps the last piece of chocolate not owned by the French.
What is that tree, he thinks, it was not there before;
but closer, it is more than a tree;
one naked man impaled on a splintered limb,
his legs and arms hacked off and hung on branches,
two others, but Goya cannot see more,
kneels at the side of the road and retches;
Is this what I was born for?

10.

It takes him years to make the plates.
Feels he is giving away gobbets of his own flesh.
Why would anyone want to do this, he asks,
then, *why can't I stop?*
The images grow inside him as they appear on the plates.
What is photography to this?
These images cut into his heart like petroglyphs
as the burin slices through the zinc.
What it costs him to make these;
more than he has, or has ever wanted.
But over the years he is lighter,
and after the dream of the dog vomiting corpses
he knows he is through. When he dies,
he thinks, he will be like a spider's husk
in an abandoned window sill,
transparent and full of light.

PART THREE

Raids on Homer

What mattered if Helen were a whore,
Or grandame of sound progeny?
Troy would still be standing, four times
The size of our own London—Hector not
Dismembered, shamed, his privates maimed,
And dodd'ring Priam's ancient head not
Dog-beslavered;
And a race of warriors in their prime
Not undone.
Quod erat demonstrandum. Of course,
We should not then have had the *Iliad*.
                    (Brecht, *Edward The Second.)*

A BAR IN ARGOS

"They'll tell you it was a wooden horse;
I'll tell you it was not.
We gutted twenty oxen,
and slid inside their empty bellies,
but for our short-swords, naked;
then were sewn up, delivered to the city gates
as an offering of peace,
acquiescent to Troy's enduring power
and that night while the cooks made the fires
to roast the beasts with us as stuffing,
we cut the rawhide sutures
and were born out of the stink and slime,
killing first the cooks, headfirst in their vats,
their legs kicking, then moving
through the streets garrotting sentries,
dowsing their torches in puddles,
killing blindly—twice killing our own—
catching Trojans in their beds,
and Odysseus ecstatic, almost forgetting
to open the city gates; the high point of his night
when with a pike he pinned a woman to her bed
right through her lover's back.
I tell you I was sick, still am, it rots your soul;
it's just that anything you think is twisted
Odysseus can give another twist
you wouldn't think was there to give.
I tell you the man's a son of a bitch.
Wooden horse? Fuck me!
We were shat out of oxen to win that war."

HOMER DOES NOT MENTION HIM

Now follow one soldier home to Argos,
not Agamemnon nor Ajax nor Diomedes
but Petros the stone-cutter with his limp
and ruined shoulder from swinging a short-sword
all those years. Lungs rotten from the choking
yellow dust, sleeping cold nights
on the plain under a spear-propped shield,
heart hard as his heels from killing.
Not the sleek, oiled body of an Achaean prince
but Petros with his overlarge head,
beard like a boar's bristles.
Home in his little village
on the gull-spattered cliffs above the sea
he waits at the door of his stone hut
for his wife to recognize him,
not as Penelope knew Odysseus disguised
but as a woman who sees a husband, only older,
something unnameable gone out of him.
And then he stammers,
We had three children when I left now there are four.
And the wind, snarling up the old road,
swirls a handful of dust over them,
a benediction against the bone-knowing
of what silence brings
beyond the clunk of the goat's bell.

FIRST BLOOD

He didn't know until he'd seen
Troy's towers spiny in the haze,
heard keel striking sand like a javelin,
that he carried the house of the fathers
on his back,
didn't know the weight of it
until he'd swung a short-sword all day
against Hector's lot, arms aching,
thighs spattered with gore,
cheek layed open by a close cut.
That night as he lay shivering awake,
he clung to these images:
the handful of olives he gave the shepherd girl,
the warmth of the Aegean as he swam
toward his father's boat with the wineskin,
the smell of the blossoming groves at home,
the lemons bright in the moonlight.

THE WAR

Paris lies in the ivory inlaid bed,
fresh from the bath, sponged and dabbed
like a baby by Aphrodite's deft hands,
olive-eyed and sleek,
a body perfectly muscled,
but not for killing; hands too soft to field a spear,
senses too fine to take
the endless shock of sword on shield;
a fate borne by him without pretension,
as if his sexuality were a long illness,
and now Helen, a victim of the same disease,
watery gown clasped beneath the breasts, hair
black fire bursting over her shoulders.
Hate, she thinks,
letting the gold clasp's weight drop
the gown around her ankles,
Paris smiling, *That is the way I like you.*
Hate, she says, *Hate,* one knee on the bed and falling forward,
but now they are lost in the sweet sickness
and Aphrodite sits by the bronze lamp and trembles,
watches the soft roundness of flesh shift and clutch,
lock and shudder, the mist of sweat
catching the flame's flicker
and Helen looks at Paris, breathing hard, *I hate you,*
and Paris says, *I hate you too,* the sound of the fighting
beyond the walls like drunken cooks,
their bronze pots falling down the stairs.

SPOKEN BY THE SENTRY
AT ACHILLES'S TENT

Why did the girl Briseis weep for Patroclus?
Taken from her father by Achilles, raped,
then seized by Agamemnon, raped again.
Then Agamemnon gave her back to bribe Achilles
to return so the sea would not froth red
with our cut throats. But upon returning to Achilles's tent
she saw Patroclus, dead, his stiffening beauty
stretched out on a cot, the demi-god insane with grief.
I watched her throw herself across the corpse and sob.
They say even Achilles's horses wept for Patroclus
by why this girl, sixteen, who could not wish
any of us well? Perhaps because she saw
her own spoiled body lying there, her ruined life.
Someday, she will be taken back to Phthia
where she will serve whomever Achilles takes as a bride.
Perhaps she will make a little sphere around her body,
a faint light visible only to slaves and other concubines
in which she'll dream a young girl running
along the sea with the surf cold on her ankles.
And perhaps she will weave the scenes into
fine cloth for her lady. Patroclus was seventeen,
the boy who speaks to you the same.
Brought here because I can put an arrow
through a halter ring at a hundred meters,
tell a hummock from a creeping man on a moonless night
but most important because I can keep my mouth shut,
my feelings hid, even what I feel now.
I Spiros, son of a sandalmaker, entrust to you this secret:
I would take her home and love her as she is,
lay my hand on her heart and leave it there
until she remembers that she has one.

DESCENT

When Achilles wakes in the underworld he sobs like a child.
How good it feels to have left his rage
stinking in that blinding, god-hammered armor.
He rubs his heel and the visions come:
Helen sending out the slaves and girdling herself
secretly before the mirror;
and even as the tents are struck for the voyage home,
Agamemnon beating a concubine
because his penis will not honor his command.
The markets of Argos filling with the crutched
and nubbled with their olive bitter mouths;
a blind hoplite lifting his robe to show
his testicles gone, people throwing money in his hat;
Clytemnestra seething, watching for Atrides's signal fires.
Rejoice, Achilles, home now in Hades.
How wise of Thetis to have held you by the heel
when she dipped you in the waters of immortality,
to have left one place on you ungodlike
that stinks of self and time.
Lie down and rest, Achilles, at last no larger and no smaller
than you are, and no shame in that.
Leave all the noise to the living;
when like a meteor you hit the atmosphere of death
all that burned up, left you as you were when you were born,
before the world conspired to make you other.

HOMECOMING

Telemachus felt something enter his spine
when his father threaded the ax-heads,
victorious arrow quivering in the wall,
and a small cry escaped him when,
without pausing, the old man fit
another shaft onto the string
and shot Antinoos between the nipples.
And so it began for Telemachus,
the deep, swirling momentum;
some power slipping him on like a skin,
and him mad with it; hiss of sword-stroke;
father and son working the cowering suitors,
the one stalking, the other cutting off escape,
until the stone floors were slippery red.
But finally, when he thought it was over,
his righteousness spent, and the weeping servant girls
on their hands and knees were sopping up the blood,
he leaned on his sword,
tried to fit his dream of the man gone twenty years
over the gore-soaked beard and chest before him.

And then his father looked around, and scarce believing
there was no one left to kill, smiled at his son.

EREBUS

You have the dream again: monsoon season, jungle,
a muddy village road; you are naked,
stumbling along a paddy dike across an open field
toward the village where C.W. killed all the pigs
but once into the trees
there is only thickening jungle,
canopy hung with smoldering flares.
You stumble into an open field,
cupping your balls,
and from the next treeline
you hear music, Motown, Aretha,
who used to throb from the mortar pits
where the brothers slung round after round down the tubes,
a little respect,
and when you enter the village, ashamed,
you see men you tagged dead
and choppered out like sides of beef,
grinning at you from around a fire,
and the old women, the children
who didn't move quick enough, all the Cong,
they are there too,
and the ones from the day so many died
you tore up your own clothes for bandages;
all there and singing, lit amber by the fire.
What took you so long, Doc, they say.
They ask you where you've been and you can't tell them.
Over twenty years since you got lost coming home,
and now you're back here in the stinking silt and hedgerows,
shin deep in pigs, but this time
naked and without a weapon.
And so you sit down with the dead.
Reese with the white eyebrows
wraps a poncho around your shoulders,
tells you what it was like when he was dying,
treeline crackling with machinegun fire

you pounding on his chest to start his heart
and him thinking, *Easy, its so quiet where I am,*
quiet and fine, and Ballard,
blue black and thick-shouldered, telling you
he watched you working on his body from above,
how you were white and sweat-soaked,
your chest heaving, trying to find the exit wound
and keep from being hit
and how he wanted to tell you it was all right,
it was fine, and Price, arms so long
he could fold a sheet by himself,
whom you crawled down into the stream bed
to drag out by the heels, lived to go home,
killed in a dope deal two years later.
All of us are here, he says, *sit down,*
we'll get you some clothes,
you're home now, easy,
remember what you used to say?
You're going to be fine, my man,
you're going home,
just don't fade out on me,
hey, what's your mother' s maiden name?

PART FOUR

Among the Monumbos of German New Guinea anyone who has slain a foe in war becomes thereby "unclean".... [He] must remain a long time in the men's club-house.... He may touch nobody, not even his own wife and children; if he were to touch them it is believed that they would be covered with sores. He becomes clean again by washing and using other modes of purification.

—Sir James Frazier, *The Golden Bough*

RAIN

1968:
For you, sitting in a barracks in Okinawa,
the war is over. You are quiet,
as if experiencing silence for the first time.
You don't know what to do. Stare at your hands.
From the barracks sergeant you obtain
the name of a place where you can be washed and massaged.
You go there in the rain.
A shy, plain woman hands you a towel,
leads you to a room where you lie on a mat.
She makes you feel like a child lifted from a basinet.
When you roll over you are hard.
There is a brief haggling to adjust the price.
She turns away from you to do it, facing your feet,
her hair in a tight little bun.
Another woman passes through, smiles at you,
the way women of your childhood bent over your pram.
You think of the lepers you saw bathing in the sea
near Monkey Mountain. When you come,
it is the priming of tears
and as she washes her hands, her back still toward you,
you cry. And the steam. And the water everywhere.
The rain outside. And life comes back.

YES

No, I said. I remember the sound,
the way it opened out in me.
Say it, *No,*
feel how it opens your throat,
down into your heart,
how it echoes.
In Vietnamese, no is *khong,*
oh again the heart's widener.
That day the word drilled through me,
drove into the ground and held me in the red mud,
where the *xa,* the spirits lived.
Corporal T., a boy with his shirt off,
vivid as a flame,
tattoo of a little red devil on his shoulder blade,
pushed the old man into a bunker,
rolled a grenade in after him
and I said *No,*
four seconds before the mortal crunch
raised dust from the hole
and it rained blood. That boy,
maddened by the heat, pea-brained,
so packed with idiocy,
no room around the hate for a breath, a question.
Wonder where he is today,
if he has found his Yes, his No.
Later I grew my hair half way down my back,
lived with Suzanne in her tepee.
How she mothered me, fed me peyote, mushrooms,
unchewable bread, and I loved her
for the whole summer after the war.
We'd sit in the Arizona night,
drink in meteor showers
and one night when stoned
she painted half my body green,
and I wobbled naked in the desert,

50

heard the mountain to the south echo, *No,*
that sound, from the ink-edged darkness on the horizon,
that mountain, that lady giant on her side,
hip framed by Cassiopeia, *yes,* that sound, *No,*
echos even now in me,
a resonance from which so many yesses come,
and I've grown to love the part of me that spoke it.

PHANTOM

She was wearing a P.O.W. bracelet
and I could not help but tell her
that when a pilot went down
the others radioed back they had seen the chute open
whether it had or not,
so families of the ones lost
would continue to receive their combat pay.
I lay awake wondering at myself,
her father's age,
and how everything is eventually revealed.
How we are blind tunneling toward
the truth tunneling toward us
and yet are always surprised to meet it in the end;
and of the pilot we found,
dangling from the tree-snagged chute,
rotting in the iridescent flightsuit
that would be there long after we were gone.
Her eyelids began to flutter near dawn
and she woke briefly to tell me that she had dreamed
of a phantom so high up
it seemed a needle glimmering in the sun,
then the missile and the bloom of gold,
shower of burning fragments
and in a few seconds, the sound,
like a fist to the heart.
And then she slept
through the noise of garbage trucks,
the tenor practicing in the airshaft,
the polyphony of alarm clocks, radios and toilets.
Any fool can tell the truth,
it takes an old heart to know how and when
and I shouldn't wonder
if I told her what I knew,
she would ask me to stay up with her
while the last flame of her father flickered out.

MUGGING, BROOKLYN, 1981

I saw the knife flash,
two whispering absences emerge
from leaves shining with mist,
then the thin pressure on my neck.
I'll cut your jugular vein,
and some far off part of me wanted to tell him
he meant *carotid artery,*
but fear squeezed my kidneys and I choked.
Pushed down the driveway behind a brownstone, robbed.
They made me climb a high fence
to put distance between us, and after,
arms cruciform,
I showed the cops the bruises
from the pickets in my palms,
White man's stigmata,
but they didn't laugh.
At the precinct with the mug book,
faces fixed to names chosen by a mother's hope:
Jesus. Mathew. Juan.
Some beaten puffy, chin up and insolent,
or onyx-eyed with dope.
They were very professional, I said.
It's their job, said the cop.
A week later, no more jokes,
puking up rage I smashed a chair,
imagining brains scattered by a crowbar.
Halfway to the hardware store to buy a machete,
I sat on a bus bench and cried.
After the war, I gave away my hunting guns.
How my life is known by glints that promise knowledge
and how with every truth the darkness seems to double.

OUTLIVING OUR GHOSTS

For Al Miller

You show me the X-ray,
tell me how the bullet clipped the rim of your helmet,
sheared off the top of your ear,
continued downward into the shoulder
where the nerves cable under the collarbone,
soft as the white of an eye, and there,
broke up and stopped. The Jews say,
Bad times past are good to tell of.
Al, did we dream it all?
With your fingers you trace bullet fragments,
how they have moved over the years
as your body continued its path toward the death
that touched your shoulder twenty years ago
and spun you back into life with your eyes open.
Flesh alive then is no longer part of us.
If each cell is new every seven years,
what is the heart's tattoo?
And the years between. You finding Buddha
in a young Vietnamese you killed;
me getting sober, seeing my life stand up
as from the tall grass,
where it had lain all this time, covered with signs.
Talking again we honor the darkness,
breathe again the sweet air of a second life.
We are here and we are whole.
I hold the X-ray up to the light:
the fragments still in your flesh,
bright winter stars.

RECOVERY

Going south on 91 after a storm,
black ice on a bridge. The car skids.
Stars above and below, headlights in fog
moving down the hill ahead.
The grip of tires and pavement and I breathe again.
I am like the man who lives beside a stream all his life,
and on the day he dies, hears it for the first time.
I want all my life back,
especially things pushed into darkness.
Inside my brain lights come on.
Like a cleaning lady moving from room to room
in an empty skyscraper against a black sky.
A flicker of fluorescence and whole years thaw out.
The Buddhist monk in the hole with me
during a rocket attack. Giggled,
because he didn't know the etiquette
for sharing a piece of Hell with a foreigner.
The smell of Arizona in May.
At sixteen I went to Mexico with a carload of drunks
to get my ashes hauled.
In a bar with no door because it never closed.
With a girl who'd been at it since morning.
Afterwards asked if she could sleep
five minutes against my shoulder. Between customers.
I will never forget the warmth of her skin,
her body like a little melon,
the crucifix between her breasts,
her false eyelash loose and moving with my breath.
All of it.

ITINERARY

In Arizona coming across the border with dope in my tires
and for months tasting the rubber in what I smoked.
With a college degree and a trunk full of the war.
Working in one place long enough to get the money
to stay high for a month and then moving on. Drinking a quart
of whiskey, then getting up, going to work the next day.
A little speed to burn off the hangover. In the afternoon
a few reds to take the edge off the speed and then to the bar.
At the bar, the madonna in the red mirror. My arm around her
waist and the shared look that said, The World Is Coming Apart,
Let Us Hold One Another Against The Great Noise Of It All.
Waking with her the next morning and seeing her older,
her three year-old wandering in and staring with a little worm
of confusion in his forehead. The banner on her bedroom wall
that read ACCEPTANCE in large block letters.
At night going out to unpack the war from my trunk.
A seabag full of jungle utilities that stank of rice paddy
silt and blood. To remind myself it happened. Lost them somewhere
between Tucson and Chicago. Days up on a scaffold
working gable-end trim with Mexicans who came through
a hole in the fence the night before. Rednecks who paid
me better than them. Laughing at jokes that weren't funny
to keep the job. At a New Braunfels Octoberfest getting in a fight
with a black army private who wore a button that read,
Kiss me I'm German. Don't remember what the fight was about.
Back in Tucson. Up against the patrol car being cuffed
for something I don't remember doing. Leaving the state.
Back with Jill in San Antonio. Finding her in the same bar,
driving her home in her car because she was too drunk.
The flashers on behind me, then the flashlight in my face.
In those gentle days they drove you home. Stealing Jill's car
out of the impoundment lot next morning to avoid the fee.
Later sitting buck-naked across from one another at the breakfast
table wondering who we were. This woman who wanted to live
with a man who had dreams so bad he would stay awake for days

until the dreams started to bleed through into real time
and he had to go back the other way into sleep to escape them.
Who woke with the shakes before dawn
and went to the kitchen for beer. Later walking down
to the barrio slowly, without talking, our hips touching.
The Mexican restaurant, a pink adobe strung with chilipepper
Christmas lights the year round. Inside, the bullfight calendar
with the matador's corpse laid out on a slab, naked and blue
with a red cloth across his loins and the inevitable grieving virgin
kneeling at his side. The wound in the same place the centurion
euthanized Christ with his spear. Our laughing then not laughing
because laughter and grief are born joined at the hip.
An old Mexican woman fanning herself at the cash register,
her wattles trembling. *Recordar:* to remember, to pass again
through the heart. Corazone. Corragio. Core.

BLUES

Love won't behave. I've tried
all my life to keep it chained up.
Especially after I gave up pleading.
I don't mean the woman,
but the love itself. Truth is,
I don't know where it comes from,
why it comes, or where it goes.
It either leaves me feeling the knife
of my first breath
or hang-dog and sick
at someone else's unstoppable
and as the blues song says,
can't sit down, stand up, lay down pain.
Right now I want it.
I'm like a country who can't remember the last war.
Well, that's not strictly true.
It's just been too long.
Too long and my heart is like
a house for sale in a lot full of high weeds.
I want to go down to New Orleans
and find the Santeria woman
who will light a whole table full of candles
and moan things, place a cigar
and a shot of whiskey in front of Chango's picture
and kiss the blue dead Jesus on the wall.
I want something.
Used to be I'd get a bottle
and drink until the lights went out
but now I carry my pain around everywhere I go
because I'm afraid
I might put it down somewhere and lose it.
I've grown tender about my mileage.
My teeth are like stonehenge and my tongue
is like an old druid fallen in a ditch.
A soul is like a shrimper's net they never haul up

and it's full of everything:
A tire. A shark. An old harpoon.
A Kid's plastic bucket.
An empty half-pint.
A broken guitar string.
A pair of ballerina's shoes with the ribbons tangled
in an anchor chain.
And the net gets heavier until the boat
starts to go down with it and you say,
God, what is going on.
In this condition I say love is a good thing.
I'm ready to capsize.
I can't even see the shoreline.
I haven't seen a seagull in three days.
I'm ready to drink salt water,
go overboard and start swimming.
Suffice it to say I want to get in the bathtub
with the Santeria woman and steam myself pure again.
The priest that blesses the water may be bored.
Hung over. He may not even bless it,
just tell people he did. It doesn't matter.
What the Santeria woman puts on it with her mind
makes it like a holy mirror.
You can float a shrimp boat on it.
The spark that jumps between her mind
and the priest's empty act
is what makes the whole thing light up
like an oilslick on fire against a sunset over Oaxaca.
So if I just step out into it.
If I just step off the high dive over a pool
that may or may not have water in it;
that act is enough
to connect the two poles of something
and make a long blue arc.
I don't have a clue about any of this.

Come on over here and love me.
I used to say that drunk.
Now I am stark raving sober
and I say, *Come on over here and love me.*

WARRIORS

When I came home from the war
I gave my hunting guns to a painter
who wanted to know about *those things,*
wanted to sit some morning waiting
for javelina to emerge from groundfog,
a gentle man who hadn't seen
what a 308 can do to a lung.
I let the screen door slam,
left him turning the things over and over
in the afternoon light,
hefting the Remington to his shoulder,
imagining the kick,
and on the way home I remembered
the chinaberry fight in the old barn,
raising welts on one another's heads with slingshots,
and afterwards
going to the house of the kid we called "Snush",
a nickname of forgotten origin,
but which sounded,
one of us said,
Like a sack of shit hitting a wall
and how, with his parents in the next room,
we just started hitting him. In the face.
And how he took it
and despite the bruises never told,
because we were the only friends he had,
and to keep us
he walked behind us
carrying all our cowardice on his back.

THE WALL

For Maya Lin

Black mirror cut into the green, from a distance seems a scar,
but closer, the crook of an arm to cradle the head,
it draws us in, embraces. A place of whispers, and tourists
wander confused, are hesitant to photograph, seeing themselves
reflected so. How are we to be, they seem to ask, and what is this?
The young ask especially, threatened by this invitation to grieve,
this knowledge of how things become one in the end, or how
this labial gesture of stone draws the surrounding monuments
into contention, shames them with the suggestion that we are not stone,
but reflections of earth, before and behind these names.
I move my finger down the index, find the name of the first man
I could not help, and for a moment, the tree splintering
in front of me, smell of blood and cordite, his lips turning blue,
the gasp of a lung filling with blood. I select more names
in order of their passing, find their places on the wall.
All along the base dried flowers scatter, some have left letters
to the dead, some medals. A young girl, too young to know this war,
sobs nonetheless, so precise are these fifty-eight thousand facts,
but we who fought there never imagined we would return to such a world,
to such a monument, numb, we did not yet imagine that for us the war
had just begun, that for years we would be picking through the shards,
the war pursuing us everywhere, our dreams, our lives with women,
chasing us from hiding place to hiding place, would wait at the edge
of whatever anesthesia's groundfog, would wait, would wait until
we looked it in the eye. My face reflected, I watch the wall's
perspective vector into earth and wonder, how long a wall,
if we inscribe three million Vietnamese, four million Cambodians,
how long a wall? And after Hiroshima and the Holocaust how if an
Asian woman turns a mirror of black granite, gazing stone of possibility,
womb of Kali, and not least, the night we wander in becoming whole.

PROSPERO

Say goodbye to the thing that dwarfs the heart.

Goodbye, like Prospero letting go spirit by spirit,
breaking his staff over his knee,
feeling the power he has relinquished
rise in him from the earth.
But watch: Miranda, unnoticed, picks up a splinter from the staff,
hides it in her sleeve.

The same dream: I am an old man
and the war is still raging.

There is a breeze off the river.
A shift in the light
as if the light is water
and someone has stirred the bottom with his feet.

Soon I will go out with the night patrol.
One man will lift the wire
and seven of us will duck under it,
walk the path through the perimeter mines,
through the sugar cane.
We will pass through the village and the people
will stop whispering in their hootches.
They will listen to our breathing,
squeak of rifle straps,
slosh of canteens.
When we have passed they will begin whispering again.

Just inside the treeline the trail takes a turn.
In the elbow of the turn
you cannot see the man in front
nor the man behind
and for a moment it is possible to be completely alone
in the jungle darkness.

All time pours into this moment:
never has there been more clarity,
more perfect simplicity.

There are questions which grow in me like embryos.

I live in dread someone asking them.

Like the earnest young woman at the reading:
If it had not been for the war,
would you have written?
I think,
look at the carpet we have woven with the hair of the dead.

I am very grateful to the following people for their encouragement
and disinterested criticism during the making of these poems:
Joan Larkin, Tim Liu, Jim Finnegan, Susan Finnegan, Linda
Gregg, Marie Howe, Chuck Martin, Margaret Lloyd, Harriet
Brickman, Roz Driscol, Anne Woodhall, Pamela Stewart, Angela
Madeiras, Rita Gabis, Kerry O'keefe, Ted Deppe, Paul Jenkins,
Gregory Orr, Martín Espada, Deborah DeNicola, Frazier Russell,
Carol Houck Smith, as well as members past and present of the
Group 18 poetry workshop, and especially, Jack Gilbert.

The author wishes to express his gratitude for grants and prizes
received from the following in support of the writing of these poems:

The National Endowment for the Arts, The Massachusetts
Cultural Council,
The Virginia Quarterly Review,
The Massachusetts Artists Foundation
The Poets & Writers, Inc. *Writers Exchange*

And to the Trustees of the Estate of Robert Francis
gratitude for my two years residency
at Fort Juniper

Recent Titles from Alice James Books:

Margaret Lloyd, *This Particular Earthly Scene*
Jeffrey Greene, *To the Left of the Worshiper*
Timothy Liu, *Vox Angelica*
Suzanne Matson, *Durable Goods*
Jean Valentine, *The River at Wolf*
David Williams, *Traveling Mercies*
Rita Gabis, *The Wild Field*
Deborah DeNicola,*Where Divinity Begins*
Richard McCann, *Ghost Letters*

Alice James Books has been publishing poetry since 1973. One of the few presses in the country that is run collectively, the cooperative selects manuscripts for publication and the new authors become active members of the press, participating in editorial and production activities. The press was named for Alice James, sister of William and Henry, whose gift for writing was ignored and whose fine journal did not appear until after her death.

Doug Anderson has written a play, *Short Timers*, a chapbook, *Bamboo Bridge*, as well as fiction and filmscripts. His critical work has appeared in the *New York Times Book Review* and the *London Times Literary Supplement*. He has received grants and awards including a fellowship from the National Endowment for the Arts, the Massachusetts Cultural  Council and The Massachusetts Artists Foundation. Poems in this collection received the Emily Balch Prize for the best poems to appear in the *Virginia Quarterly Review* in 1993. He teaches writing and literature at Mt. Wachusett Community College in Gardner, Massachusetts.